A NOTE TO PARENTS

When your children are ready to "step into reading," giving them the right books is as crucial as giving them the right food to eat. **Step into Reading Books** present exciting stories and information reinforced with lively, colorful illustrations that make learning to read fun, satisfying, and worthwhile. They are priced so that acquiring an entire library of them is affordable. And they are beginning readers with a difference—they're written on five levels.

Early Step into Reading Books are designed for brand-new readers, with large type and only one or two lines of very simple text per page. **Step 1 Books** feature the same easy-to-read type as the Early Step into Reading Books, but with more words per page. **Step 2 Books** are both longer and slightly more difficult, while **Step 3 Books** introduce readers to paragraphs and fully developed plot lines. **Step 4 Books** offer exciting nonfiction for the increasingly independent reader.

To all the dedicated teachers
who help and inspire their students.
—J.H.

Dedicated to my mother,
Evelyn Dagny Konrad, who taught me compassion.
—N.C.

Text copyright © 1997 by Johanna Hurwitz
Illustrations copyright © 1997 by Neverne Covington
All rights reserved under International and Pan-American Copyright
Conventions. Published in the United States by Random House, Inc., New York,
and simultaneously in Canada by Random House of Canada Limited, Toronto.

http://www.randomhouse.com/

Library of Congress Cataloging-in-Publication Data
Hurwitz, Johanna. Helen Keller : courage in the dark / by Johanna Hurwitz ;
illustrated by Neverne Covington. p. cm. – (Step into reading, a Step 3 book)
SUMMARY: A biography of the blind and deaf girl who overcame both handicaps
with the help of her teacher, Annie Sullivan.
ISBN 0-679-87705-3 (pbk.) – ISBN 0-679-97705-8 (lib. bdg.)
1. Keller, Helen, 1880–1968–Juvenile literature.
2. Blind-deaf–United States–Biography–Juvenile literature.
3. Sullivan, Annie, 1866–1936–Juvenile literature.
[1. Keller, Helen, 1880–1968. 2. Blind. 3. Deaf. 4. Physically handicapped.
5. Sullivan, Annie, 1866–1936. 6. Women–Biography.]
I. Title. II. Series: Step into reading. Step 3 book.
HV1624.K4H88 1997 362.4'1'092–dc20 [B] 96-38206

Printed in the United States of America 10 9 8 7 6 5 4 3 2 1

STEP INTO READING is a registered trademark of Random House, Inc.

Step into Reading®

HELEN KELLER
COURAGE IN THE DARK

by Johanna Hurwitz

illustrated by Neverne Covington

A Step 3 Book

Random House 🏠 New York

Chapter 1

Helen Keller was born on June 27, 1880, on a farm in Alabama.

Mr. and Mrs. Keller were thrilled with their beautiful, healthy baby. But then something terrible happened.

When little Helen was a year and a half old, she became very sick. She had a high fever. Her parents were afraid that she would die.

A few days later, the fever was gone. But something was still very wrong. Little Helen could no longer see or hear. The illness had left her blind and deaf.

The Kellers' sweet little girl became a wild child. She kicked and scratched her parents when they tried to touch her.

She yelled and screamed in a loud voice. How else could she let anyone know when she was hungry or tired or afraid?

Mealtime was terrible for the Keller family. Helen stuck her hands into everyone's food. She threw things across the dinner table.

Helen did whatever she wanted. Her parents could not make her behave.

Once, Helen woke in the middle of the night. Since she could not see, she thought it was morning. Mrs. Keller tried to put her daughter back to bed. But Helen insisted on getting up and getting dressed. Then she went into the kitchen. Though it was nighttime, she screamed for her breakfast.

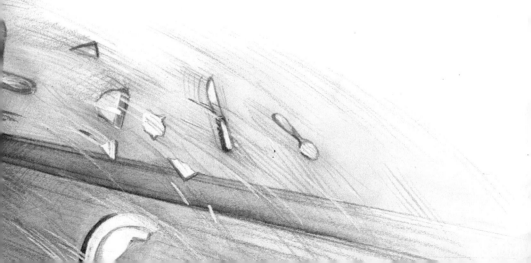

Helen's parents did not know what to do. They wanted to help their little girl. But how? They did not know any blind or deaf people. They did not know where to turn for help.

One day, Mrs. Keller heard about Dr. Chisholm. He was a special eye doctor in Baltimore, Maryland. Some of his patients were blind and deaf, just like Helen. For the first time, Mrs. Keller felt a little bit of hope. Maybe Dr. Chisholm could help Helen. The Kellers took their daughter to Baltimore right away.

Dr. Chisholm could not cure Helen. But he told the Kellers not to worry. He said that even a blind child could learn many things. He sent them to Washington to meet Alexander Graham Bell.

Mr. Bell invented the telephone. And because his own wife was deaf, he knew a

great deal about teaching deaf people.
Mr. Bell told the Kellers about the Perkins
Institution for the Blind. The Perkins

Institution was a special school in Boston, Massachusetts. One of its students was a girl named Laura Bridgman. Like Helen, Laura was both blind and deaf. Teachers at Perkins taught her how to sew.

Mr. Bell said that a teacher from Perkins might be able to help Helen.

The Kellers' hopes soared.

Chapter 2

Mr. and Mrs. Keller wrote a letter to the Perkins Institution. A teacher wrote back. Her name was Anne Sullivan. Friends called her Annie.

Annie agreed to come and live with the Kellers and to teach Helen. Helen was now almost seven years old.

On March 3, 1887, Annie moved to Alabama. It would turn out to be the most important day of Helen's life.

As a child, Annie had been almost blind herself. Luckily, several operations helped her see again. But Annie never forgot what it was like to be blind. She hoped she would be able to help young Helen.

Right away, Annie saw that Helen was a tall, pretty girl. But she also saw that Helen was not happy. She almost never smiled.

Helen could not understand the world around her. She lived in darkness and silence. She could not tell people how she felt. No wonder she was so unhappy!

At first Helen was not a good student. She did not obey Annie. Helen was used to having her own way. Her parents had allowed her to act out. They never punished her. They thought she could not control her behavior.

Annie had to teach Helen everything. She was very strict with her young student. Helen was strong and stubborn—but so was Annie. Sometimes Helen pinched or hit Annie. When Helen hit her, Annie hit her back. Bit by bit, Helen learned to pay attention to her new teacher.

Annie taught Helen many new things.
She taught her to sit at the dinner table.
She taught her to eat with a knife and fork
and spoon. She taught her to dress herself
and brush her hair.

Annie wanted to teach her student
something that was even more important.
She wanted to teach young Helen how to
understand words.

At the Perkins Institution, Annie had learned a special finger alphabet. Different hand positions stood for different letters. She could speak to deaf people by spelling out words with her hands.

Helen had lost her sense of sight and her sense of hearing. But she still had her

sense of touch. Annie tried to teach Helen the special alphabet.

She spelled out one word after another inside Helen's hand. Helen copied Annie and repeated the finger movements. She learned how to spell *doll, cake, milk,* and *mug.* But she did not understand what the words meant. Annie tried over and over, but Helen still did not understand.

One spring day, Annie and Helen went for a walk outside. Annie took Helen to a well. The teacher pumped some water and let it run over Helen's fingers. Slowly she spelled out the word *water* into Helen's palm. Then she did it again and again.

Suddenly, the little girl understood.
The wet liquid and the word being spelled
in her palm were the same thing! WATER.

After that, Helen was quick to learn other words. One day she learned thirty new words.

Annie Sullivan was proud of her student. She could not believe how quickly Helen learned. Helen wanted to know everything. She had discovered a whole new exciting world.

Annie called Helen's progress a miracle. Her accomplishments were amazing. She had done the impossible.

Helen now knew how to express her thoughts. For the first time, she was happy. The crying fits stopped. Whenever Annie taught her a new word, Helen threw her arms around her teacher and kissed her.

Chapter 3

In May 1888, Helen was ready for a new challenge. Shortly before her eighth birthday, she went to Boston with Annie. They went to Annie's old school, the Perkins Institution. There Helen learned to read Braille.

Braille is a form of writing. It was
invented in France by a blind man named
Louis Braille. Patterns of raised dots stand
for each letter of the alphabet. Using the
Braille system, blind people can *feel* the
letters with their fingertips. With this
wonderful alphabet, Helen learned to read!

Helen already loved words. Now she loved the stories that words could tell. She read many, many books. And then, using a special Braille typewriter, she wrote some stories of her own.

There was so much that Helen could learn at the Perkins Institution. Soon she and Annie began to spend winters in Boston and summers at home in Alabama.

When Helen was ten years old, she met another teacher in Boston. Her name was

Sarah Fuller. Sarah wanted to teach Helen
how to speak.

Until then, Helen could speak only with
her fingers. She could talk only to people
who understood the special hand language
that Annie had taught her. Sarah wanted
to teach Helen to speak with her mouth.

First Helen moved her hand over Sarah's face. She felt Sarah's lips and tongue when she spoke. Then Helen copied these movements. She tried to make sounds. Helen's first *spoken* sentence was "It is warm."

It took a long, long time for Helen to improve her speech. She had to practice very hard. At first, only Annie and Sarah could understand what Helen said. Annie had to repeat Helen's words so others could understand, too.

But Helen was determined to speak on her own. She would not give up. Eventually, she learned how to speak more clearly. When Helen spoke, everyone listened!

Helen learned something else at the Perkins Institution. She learned how to read people's lips.

She could not actually see people's lips moving. But she could feel them with her fingers. By placing her hands on the lips and throat of a speaker, Helen could figure out what was being said.

Everyone was amazed at what Helen had learned. She was one of the first blind and deaf people to speak aloud and understand spoken words.

Chapter 4

When Helen was fourteen, she attended the Wright-Humason School for the Deaf in New York City. The school helped her improve her speech and lip-reading skills. Using the hand alphabet and Braille, Helen also learned German and French.

But that wasn't enough for Helen. She had a new goal. Helen wanted to go to college. She wanted to study with students who could see and hear.

For three years, Helen worked very hard to prepare for the entrance exams. The tests were copied into Braille so that Helen could read them. She worried that she might not pass. Then one day, a letter with the good news arrived. Helen had been accepted to Radcliffe College!

Helen went to Radcliffe in the fall of 1900. In class, Annie Sullivan sat at Helen's side. She spelled the professor's words into Helen's hand. Helen wrote her assignments in Braille. She was an excellent student.

Helen majored in English and German at college. She graduated with honors.

Once, she couldn't express herself at all. Now she could understand and speak several languages. Little Helen had grown into a beautiful, educated woman.

While Helen was still in college, an editor from *Ladies' Home Journal* magazine asked Helen to write about her life. Those articles were published in 1902.

Soon after, Helen wrote about herself again. She wrote a book called *The Story of My Life*. Of course, it was only a small part of her life. She was only twenty-two years old when it was published!

People all over the world wanted to read Helen's story. The book sold thousands of copies.

Chapter 5

Everybody wanted to know Helen! Helen and Annie began traveling all over the world. Helen visited Europe, Egypt, Australia, and Japan. She gave speeches about helping blind people. She wanted to reach anyone who had given up hope.

During her life, Helen met many famous people: Alexander Graham Bell, Mark Twain, Charlie Chaplin, President and Mrs. Franklin D. Roosevelt, President John F. Kennedy, and many others. They were all eager to meet Helen.

One man who met her said that Helen was like a "charge of electricity." He was overwhelmed by Helen's energy and spirit.

In 1953, Helen met President Dwight D. Eisenhower. She asked the president if she could touch his face. She wanted to use her fingers to *see* him. President Eisenhower agreed. Helen touched his mouth.

"You have a beautiful smile," she told him.

"But not much hair," the president replied.

Of course, Helen's fingers would have *seen* that, too!

Helen was an amazing person. Never before had a blind and deaf person done so much.

Even though she could not hear music, Helen learned to dance. She also attended concerts. Although she could not hear the sounds, she felt the vibrations of the music.

She went horseback riding and played with her dogs. Helen also loved to work in her garden. Though she never saw the flowers she grew, she enjoyed their scent.

Helen Keller was proof that people can do almost anything. Even people with a physical problem or handicap can reach their goals.

Helen Keller died on June 1, 1968. It was just a few weeks before her eighty-eighth birthday.

Helen's story has been retold over and over. She has been the subject of books, plays, films, and television programs. The United States Postal Service has dedicated a stamp to her. And an organization with her name works to help blind people.

Helen Keller's life was filled with silence and darkness. But she had the courage and determination to light her days.

THE BRAILLE ALPHABET

a	b	c	d	e	f

g	h	i	j	k

l	m	n	o	p

q	r	s	t	u

v	w	x	y	z